EDITED BY KITTY HARMON • PHOTOGRAPHS BY HEATHER GILSON
FOREWORD BY VICTOR LARSON

Up To NO GOOD

the rascally things boys do

as told by perfectly decent grown men

CHRONICLE BOOKS

SAN FRANCISCO

With a bang on the ear to John, the original rascal.

KH

Library of Congress Cataloging-in-Publication data available.

ISBN 0-8118-2688-0

All photographs except those on the endsheets and
     pages 2–9 by Heather Gilson
Book design by Jane Jeszeck, Jigsaw Seattle
Typeset in Avant Garde, Courier, Futura, and Gill Sans
Printed in Singapore

Distributed in Canada by Raincoast Books
8680 Cambie Street
Vancouver, B.C. V6P 6M9

10 9 8 7 6 5 4 3 2 1

Chronicle Books
85 Second Street
San Francisco, CA 94105

www.chroniclebooks.com

NEVER PASS A BOY WITHOUT THINKING ABOUT HIM.

—Australian proverb

FOREWORD

So we got this fishing line and strung it across the street late at night. In the middle of the string, about the level of a car windshield, we taped an egg. Then we waited and watched. The car approached, the egg splattered, and we congratulated ourselves on a job well done.

I had not thought about that night in years. Then I read *Up to No Good: The Rascally Things Boys Do*, and a whole world of growing up rushed back to me in vivid detail. It brought back the thrills of independent exploration and pushing boundaries. The magnetic pull to play with fire, break glass, throw rocks at things. The urge to torment others: insects, siblings, teachers, other kids. The risks we took in order to satisfy intense curiosity, bond with other boys, or generate attention. And the disgrace—and

sometimes relief—of getting caught and enduring the punishment.

All of these experiences are part of our development, preparing us to join the adult world. How interesting it is that once we enter that world, we forget the way we got there. In my work as a family therapist and developmental consultant, I advise parents on how to keep alive their connections with their kids. I spend a lot of time reminding fathers of their own childhoods; I take them back to their identity struggles and the attendant petty crimes and misdemeanors they commit-ted along the path of self-definition.

If parents remain overly concerned about a son's mischievous tendencies, I can always offer the historical context. For there is a long, fine tradition of boyhood misbehavior. I refer not to the relatively

recent span from Bart Simpson through
Dennis the Menace to the Little Rascals,
or even to pre-television scamps like the
father of our country (who, I'm sure, didn't
cut down the cherry tree so he could tell
the truth about it). In western culture we can
go back at least as far as the fourth century

B.C., when Plato asserted that "Of all the animals, the boy is the

most unmanageable."

In *The Iliad,* Homer compared the charging Trojans to
wasps from a roadside nest "when boys have made it their sport
to set them seething, day after day tormenting them round their
wayside hive—idiot boys! they make a menace for every man in
sight." And Shakespeare, in *King Lear,* reminded us that "As flies
to wanton boys, are we to the gods; They kill us for their sport."
Perhaps the boys whose stories about tormenting bees and flies

are included in this book will be dismayed to know just how common their experiences are. Or, perhaps, they will take pleasure in having played their part in a continuum of aggravating not just insects, but also their elders.

As adults we can, and probably should, wag our fingers and muse on the meaning of such misdeeds. We certainly cannot condone them. For without the risk of punishment the pranks would not be half as meaningful for the pranksters. In fact, getting caught—or the avoidance of it—is a major part of the point of such foolishness. As boys, we know the limits of the world through action. It is in the doing of the forbidden that a large measure of the world is known to us. Does this mean that we shall grow up to be maladjusted men? Some would argue as much, but would overstate the case. To develop as whole adults

we seem to require our peers to egg us on and grown-ups to reel us in at one and the same time.

Despite all our transgressions, most of us turned out just fine and find the annoying pranks of our sons perplexing—that is, unless we can remember our own. So while I wouldn't advise giving a copy of this book to a boy, I feel it can be an effective means of feeling better about his behavior. To readers who are parents of boys: If you're able to laugh at these stories, you can take solace that your perspective is intact. To everyone: Read this book with a fond eye to both the past and present generations of boys who were and are Up to No Good.

—Victor Larson, M.S.W.

In fifth grade I developed this major crush on a sixth-grader named Wendy. She always had the prettiest face and the nicest smile; everybody thought so. So I started kissing rocks and throwing them at her.

—John, Connecticut, b. 1959

I suppose every guy can tell about killing his first frog with a BB gun. When my friends and I killed one we felt a lot of remorse and decided to have a burial service. But then it grew and became quite elaborate. In school we had been learning about Egyptian tombs and decided to make this a real ceremonial burial. We made the dead frog the king, and we caught a bunch of other frogs to be his slaves in the afterlife. So the one frog we felt guilty about killing got a great burial; the other frogs died a horrible death because we buried them alive. We became hardened in no time.

—Jeb, Texas, b. 1958

13

Every summer I got together with my cousins who lived on a big farm in Iowa. I spent most of my time with "the twins," who were about my age, and for two weeks we were inseparable—playing Tom Sawyer and Huck Finn on a small crick, rodeo men trying to ride the backs of pigs, and so on.

A favorite pastime was to torment another cousin, Mick, who was two years younger and lived in California. One trick was to go out into the middle of the cow pasture and then sprint back to the barn. Since we were older we could always get about twenty or thirty yards ahead of Mick, at which point we'd yell back: "Hurry up, Mick, the bull is running after you! He's about to gore you!" Mick would be running and sobbing. Poor guy.

Then there was the electric fence
that kept the cows in the pasture. I had my first
lesson in physics when I touched the fence and felt
a strong thump in my arm from the electric shock. I
had the bright idea to try and get Mick to pee on
the fence. I told him that it felt really great to
have the electricity run through the urine up into
your penis. Mick really wanted to be part of our
gang, so he went ahead and peed on the fence. He
let out a big yell and ran away holding his
"thumped" penis. These days I'm careful not to men-
tion the words "cow" or "electricity" around Mick.

—Charlie, New York, b. 1960

One summer on Cape Cod my grandmother was about to go nuts because the crows were making such a racket that she couldn't take her afternoon nap. So she told me she'd pay me a dollar—which was a lot of money to a boy then—for every dead crow I brought her. I had an old pellet gun, and after sitting in a tree for hours I finally got lucky and shot one and brought it in to my grandmother, who was very proud of me and gave me my dollar. Then the next day I fished the dead crow out of the garbage and brought it in again, and got another dollar. I did this every day for about a week, until that crow just reeked and my grandmother figured it out. She gave me a stern lecture, but she sort of had a little smile on her face, and she didn't make me give the money back.

—John, Massachusetts, b. 1909

We used to catch fireflies and write our names on the sidewalk with them.

—Michael, Maryland, b. 1950

Every year fireflies—also known as lightning bugs—would appear around June. My friends and I went out at night with our Wiffle bats and swung at them to see who could get the biggest patch of dead, but still glowing, bugs on his bat. Sometimes we collected a lot of them and smeared them on our arms and faces so that they would glow, too. This was a great way to gross out the girls in the neighborhood.

—John, Illinois, b. 1954

It was a big deal when the movie *American Graffiti* came to our town. Everyone was planning to go. My friends and I—we were all about fourteen—got together at dusk with big jars and caught as many fireflies as we could and then snuck them into the theater. We sat in the front row of the balcony, and when they turned out the lights and started the movie we opened the jars and shook them out. They flew everywhere, blinking on and off. They had this really distinctive smell, too—sort of musky. But people thought it was great, and we probably would have gotten away with it, except we got the church giggles really bad. Then one of my friends ate a Jujyfruit with a lightning bug on it and had to spit it out, which made us laugh even harder, until we got kicked out.

—Willie, Connecticut, b. 1958

When I was ten, my parents had our kitchen remodeled. My friend Mitch and I really didn't like the job foreman. He was a grump and always yelling at us. Near the end of the job, we took a can of ginger ale, shook it up as hard as we could, and opened it up in the kitchen. It went all over the ceiling, leaving brownish stains all over this new coat of white paint. My mother came in and chewed out the foreman for doing such a bad job. We watched through the window as he stood there perplexed, trying to figure out what had gone wrong with this batch of paint. We never got caught. I remember feeling a surge of power, that two kids could pull one over on adults and get revenge for being treated like—well, like the punks that we were. We congratulated ourselves for days.

—Doug, New York, b. 1959

24

Once I took packets of ketchup and poked holes in one end with pins. Then I put them under the toilet seat, under those little knobs at the front, so that when my sister sat down ketchup squirted all over her legs.

—Willie, Connecticut, b. 1958

Once when my sister was baby-sitting my brother and me, we tied her to a chair next to the stove and put the tea kettle on to boil. There was nothing she hated more than the sound of a loud whistle. So we left her there and went outside to play.

—Bob, Ohio, b. 1938

In our neighborhood we had to rake all of our leaves out to the curb for a truck to collect. In first grade my friends and I hid under the leaf pile right before the bus came, and skipped school three days in a row. We'd go down to the beach and fish all day. My parents would say, "How'd you get so dirty at school today?" Eventually they figured it out. We got a spanking from the principal, and my dad gave me a lecture. "What if a car had run over you when you were in the leaf pile?" That gave me another idea. We buried big rocks and cinder blocks in the leaf piles, and sure enough someone blew out a tire coming too close to the curb. I learned something from that punishment, though not what my dad had intended.

—Owen, Massachusetts, b. 1958

When I was about eleven I found a bucket of gasoline in my Dad's garage. I wanted to see what would happen if I threw a match into it. I thought it would shoot this cool column of fire straight up. So I carried the bucket out into a field next to our house and threw in the match. Thankfully, I didn't catch fire. The fire shot out in a line straight back along where I had spilled the gas on my way out. It was a dry field and I was stamping the burning grass, but it was getting completely out of control. I ran up to my house where my older sister was in the yard sunbathing. I was trying to look like I wasn't panicking while I grabbed the garden hose. I walked by her calmly, then took off running once I was past her and yanked the faucet right out of the house. Huge water fountain behind me. I didn't know

which problem to deal with. My sister seemed to
think the water was a big problem, but she didn't
know about the fire yet. When I ran back out to the
field, a big fire truck pulled up. They said
they were just passing on the highway and thought I
might need some water. They got out the big hose
and now this got my sister's attention. I was still
trying to be nonchalant with her, like: "Hmmmmm,
what happened here?" Well, they put out the fire and
got back in the truck to go. We had a wraparound
driveway, and just as they were pulling out, my
parents drove in the other side. They never saw the
fire truck. As they were getting out of the car I
was begging my sister not to tell them about the
fire. So I got in trouble for the geyser shoot-
ing out of the side of the house. They never found
out about the fire.

—Gilbert, Colorado, b. 1966

When I was a kid I was pretty shy, or mean and nasty, depending on your perspective. I preferred to think of myself as a tough, boy-of-few-words, Lash Larue kind of a guy. The worst thing for me was when our parents left and we had a baby-sitter. I couldn't stand strangers in our house, especially girl strangers. When the baby-sitter arrived I went upstairs to my room and locked the door. Sometimes my parents would be gone for a while. Rather than come downstairs and see the baby-sitter, I rigged up a pulley system outside my room and lowered a cigar box through the banister to my little brother, who would fill it with food for me. This went on for a long time. In fact, I didn't lay eyes on one baby-sitter for the entire year she sat for us. She was responsible for me, but she never even knew what I looked like.

—Jim, Seattle, b. 1947

In seventh grade, the biology teacher had us dissect fetal pigs. My friends and I pocketed the snout of a pig and stuck it on the water fountain so that the water shot straight up out of the pig's nostrils. No one really noticed it until they were bent over just about to drink. The problem is that we wanted to stick around and see the results, but then we started laughing so hard that we got caught. We all got the paddle for that.

—Mark, Ohio, b. 1960

Our favorite thing was to build a man. We'd use a Styrofoam wig mold for the head, stuff old clothes with newspapers, and safety-pin him together. Behind our house was a busy road with a chain-link fence on both sides and a pedestrian overpass above it. We'd go up on the overpass and beat the tar out of the dummy and throw it off, or we'd put a noose around it so that it dangled right over the cars. All these people would screech to a stop and get out of their cars to see if the guy was all right. We'd take off running, and they couldn't chase us because of the fence. We were pretty bad. Sometimes as many as ten cars would stop. I have to say, it was awfully fun.

—Curt, Alberta, b. 1960

My brother did the same thing one time! It was on Halloween night, and he and his friends thought it would be a great stunt to make a dummy and throw it onto the highway. But they used one of my father's military shirts with his name printed on it. About an hour after they ran home, the police came to our door. All they had to do was look us up in the phone book.

—Susan, about her brother Ed, Florida, b. 1943

35

We developed several techniques for killing ants. Of course there was the old standby, the firecracker in the ant hole. You have fun watching the ants above ground run around like crazy, and imagine what's going on below the ground. It was more fun killing individual ants, though. The magnifying glass would practically melt them, with a little stream of smoke coming up. From this we developed the "sticky fry." We would leave out orange juice to attract the ants. Then we'd take a Popsicle stick and push them into the orange juice to get them really sticky, and in the meantime we'd have a lightbulb heating up. When our spit sizzled on the bulb, we'd drop the sticky ants onto the bulb and watch them shrivel. To see an ant dance, we would take the bulb out of the lamp and drop the ant into the socket. Eventually the ant would hit the terminal just right and—zzzzt.

—John, Connecticut, b. 1959

38

Lou was playing with some friends and decided to try flying. So they climbed up onto the roof of the barn, and Lou strapped some heavy wooden boards onto his brother's arms. Then they counted down, and he jumped. He was lying on the ground, groaning in pain with several broken bones, and Lou yelled down, "Hey Shorty! You forgot to flap your wings!"

—Matt, about his grandfather Lou, Wyoming, b. 1899

When my twin brother and I were four, our mother read *Mary Poppins* to us. We liked the idea of using an umbrella to fly, so we climbed up on the roof with one. Just as my brother convinced me to jump, Mother came around the corner and told us to freeze. Then she explained to us that Mary Poppins had a very special umbrella, and that ours wasn't.

—Mansfield, California, b. 1929

I grew up in Pennsylvania, but my family moved to Texas for a year or two. When we returned to Pennsylvania I went to Boy Scout camp with my old Troop 112. I had always hated the requirements of working on merit badges and moving up the ranks. So I claimed that while I was in Texas I had earned the rank of Life Scout, one rank short of Eagle. I made up some Texas-sounding merit badges I had earned, like lasso roping and bareback riding. And it worked. I didn't have to lift a finger at camp. In fact, I became bored and that always leads to trouble.

One day I was playing with matches behind a tent and discovered that when I lit the frayed ends of the tent ropes, they would smolder and throw up a lot of smoke. Around this time some

young scouts were being initiated into the Order
of the Arrow, a highly ritualized, pseudo-Indian
process involving twenty-four hours of sworn
silence and isolation in a sort of sweat-lodge
ceremony. That year's initiate from our troop was
a real suck-up, so I gathered some of my pals and
suggested how fun it would be if we could make him
break his vow of silence. My idea was to
surround Johnny's tent, light the ends of the
ropes, and yell FIRE, and then take off through
the woods when he came out screaming. So we did.
The only problem was that the tent did catch on
fire. Johnny came out screaming. An investigation
resulted in my permanent banning from the troop,
and I was sent home with my tail between my legs.

—Chad, Pennsylvania, b. 1953

When I was five I was a real tomboy, and my best friend was a neighbor boy named Bo who had a dog named Bozo. He also had a great tree house. Once we were playing up there and he talked me into trading clothes with him, underwear and all. This sounded fun to me, because I loved his suede pants with the fringe down the legs. When I was naked he got another idea. He talked me into hanging my behind over the side of the tree fort so that he could throw rocks up at me and try to get them to stick in the crack of my butt. Believe it or not, some of them did. When I went home I was excited to tell my mother about this amazing feat, but when she saw me in his clothes, she freaked out. Somehow I knew it probably wasn't a good idea to tell her about the pebbles in my bum after all.

—Samantha, about her neighbor Bo, California, b. 1949

46

My brother and I tortured our mother. We used to put a rubber band around the handle of the dish sprayer, so that when she turned on the faucet the water would spray all over the place and she would get soaked. We would ask her for a glass of water and then stand back and laugh our heads off. We used to make paper airplanes and put her pins at the points. Then when she bent over to load the dishwasher we would send them flying into her behind. These tricks were always my brother's ideas, but I went along with them because I never wanted Mom to be bored in the kitchen.

—Willie, Connecticut, b. 1958

48

A gang of boys in our neighborhood—we were all about seven or eight—used to play with this little terrier that belonged to an old lady down the street. We discovered that we could make his penis come out, all pink and shiny, and we found that fascinating. After a while it became evident that the dog was enjoying it, too. We didn't know anything about masturbation, but we knew that what we were doing was wrong. One day his penis came out all the way and wouldn't go back in. We were sure that it was permanent, and we lived in terror of getting caught.

—Michael, Minnesota, b. 1948

52

When I was young, I would climb trees looking for nests with eggs. I would watch the nests until the eggs hatched, and then I would tie a string to the chicks' legs and tie it to the tree. Then, when they were grown and ready to leave the nest, I'd go and collect them. Sometimes we kept them as pets. Sometimes we would build a fire and roast them on sticks and eat them.

—Eric, South Africa, b. 1960

I am blind, and as a kid sometimes I played with other blind kids. And we always found just as many, or more, ways to get into trouble as sighted boys. Like the time I was over at a blind friend's house, and he took me into the garage to show me his older brother's motorcycle. We decided to take it out for a spin; why not?

We rode down the street feeling for the curb, and at each intersection we'd stop, turn off the engine and listen, and then cross. We rode all the way to the high school track, where we could really let loose. First we piled up some dirt at the turns of the track so we'd feel the bump and know we were still on the track. Then we took off, going faster and faster and having a blast. What we didn't know was that people showed up to run on the track and were trying to wave us off. We couldn't hear them over the roar of the motorcycle engine, and nearly ran them over. They called the police, who showed up and tried to wave us over, too, but we kept going. Finally they got their sirens and bullhorns going and we stopped. They were furious and wouldn't believe us when we explained that we hadn't seen them. We proved we were blind by showing them our braille watches, and they escorted us home.

—Mike, California, b. 1953

55

We lived on a cul-de-sac at the bottom of a big hill. My brother was rebuilding a VW bug and had pulled the engine out. One day a friend and I decided to push the car up the hill and ride it down like a coaster. It was a blast until we came to the bottom and I went to hit the brakes, but I hit the clutch instead. We went straight into our driveway as I pulled on the parking brake, but with all that momentum we kept going—into the garage and out through the back wall. We knocked over a post supporting the main beam holding up the house, so the roof sagged. Right away we got busy and nailed the post back up, and then my mother got home. When she found out everyone was OK, she said, "Good. I always wanted a window in the garage." I learned a lot of carpentry skills after that incident. Auto bodywork skills, too.

—Dave, Washington, b. 1952

My father owned a hotel, and my friends and I would take turns stealing car keys off the parking board when no one was looking. Then we'd go out and drive around, even though we were only about thirteen. We'd return and slip the keys back and no one knew the difference, until one time when I drove a car through a fence. That could have been because we also stole an inch out of each of the bottles of liquor in the hotel bar when no one was watching.

—Donny, Ireland, b. 1966

My friends and I had a favorite empty lot in our neighborhood where we played. Every summer someone would come in with a bulldozer and strip the lot of all its vegetation. One year, I found this military manual my father had at home. He was in the National Guard and they had to learn all these military maneuvers, like building traps. So that year we decided to trap the bulldozer. We dug a five-foot-deep pit and camouflaged it with branches and leaves and dirt. I wished I had skipped school so I could have seen the bulldozer operator's face when his machine tipped over sideways into the pit. Luckily he wasn't hurt. And I learned an important lesson: If you have boys, you can never successfully hide anything in your home.

—Bill, California, b. 1949

There was this guy who knew a million ways to gross you out, like turning his eyelids inside out, belching on command, and so on. But the worst, or best, depending on how you looked at it, was what he called nose flossing. He'd take a string and shove it up his nose and then somehow work it through his sinuses, coughing and swallowing, and down into his mouth. Then he'd hold each end of the string and pull it back and forth. He'd be gagging but also giggling, because it sort of tickled. I wonder what that guy's like now. Maybe he still flosses his nose, as a parlor trick.

—Kevin, about his classmate Kyle, Washington, b. 1952

You take a sock and fill it with chalk, and then
hammer it to a powder. Then you wallop someone with
it, and their clothes get covered with dust. —Ed
• You take the long, hollow pod from a catalpa
tree and light it and pretend you're smoking.
—John • You take a can and nail holes in it and
attach a wire handle. Then you fill it with coals,
hang it on a stick, and swing it around at night,
so that sparks fly everywhere. —Ciro • You
collect green apples and bore a hole through the
middle. Then you take a long, green stick, like six
or eight feet long, and put the apple on the end.
Then you can whip the apple at your enemies. —Joe
• You take old eggs and let them sit in the sun
for a few weeks and get really rotten, and then you
lob them through the open windows of the bus as it
passes. —Joel • You attach razor blades, or

pieces of broken glass, or even broken clamshells to your kite string so you can cut the other boys' kite strings. —Freddy • You save a straw from lunch and use it for firing spitballs when the teacher's back is turned. —Jacques • You take a horseshoe nail and pound it over a bug so that the bug's guts squish out the sides. —Michael • You put rocks inside of apples and feed them to the cows, just to see that look of total confusion when they chew into them. —Andrew • You tie a scarf around a cat's belly, and it totally loses its balance. It tries to walk but keeps falling over and can't seem to control its back legs. —Steve • You go out at night and pee on the road, spinning in a circle. Then in the morning you go out and look at the stains to see how far you reached. —Juan

63

When I pulled up in front of our house the other day, the two neighbor boys were out on the sidewalk with a bunch of stuff they were selling. I went over for a look. There was a lot of really good stuff, like software, books, CDs, for really cheap. I asked how they were doing, and they said, "Great! We've sold a ton of stuff!" I picked out some art books and CDs, each for a quarter, and gave them a ten dollar bill. They had to run inside to ask their dad for change. He came outside and blew his lid when he realized what they were selling. Apparently they had asked him in a busy moment if they could have a little yard sale, and he said yes. Then they cleaned out the house.

—Jane, about her neighbors

Louis, b. 1988, and Cameron, b. 1990, Washington

When we were seven or so we learned the best
swear words from a man who was famous for it,
a farmer who rode a donkey through town every day
when it was just getting dark. Our gang of boys
would hide in the trees, waiting with our weapons.
We took strips of paper and rolled them into cone
shapes, sealed them closed with spit, and then put
a straight pin in the ends. Then we loaded them into
long pieces of plastic pipe that were our blowguns.
Finally the farmer would come along, sitting peace-
fully on top of a huge load on the donkey. Someone
would give the signal, and TAC TAC TAC TAC—the
donkey would get ten needles in the rump. The donkey
would kick and buck, with the farmer
hanging on and swearing the longest string you can
imagine. "Son of a mother of a"—well, I would
translate, but it just sounds better in Italian.

—Ciro, Italy, b. 1956

69

When we were thirteen or so my friends and I had this game. We'd go down to the basement where it was completely dark, and each of us would find a hiding place. Then someone would start the game by turning out the lights, and we'd try to hit each other with darts. You'd think you heard someone make a noise, and you'd come out of your hiding place throwing darts—but cringing because you were fair game, too. There would be complete silence, and then you'd hear someone yell, "Ow!" One time we turned on the light and a guy had a dart dangling from his cheek just below his eye. After that we wore goggles.

—Jim, Wyoming, b. 1957

My brother used to convince my little sister, who was about five, to put on her roller skates and skate around while he threw darts at her. She got pretty good at dodging the darts, so he threw them harder and harder, so hard that he finally ended up breaking a glass door. That was the end of that game.

—Shawn, about her brother Kevin, Washington, b. 1963

We used to sit in a circle and spit at the ceiling. The idea was to make your spit stick up there. If it didn't, it would land on the boy across from you, who would try to dodge it. One guy was amazing. He could make it stick every time. It would dangle up there—going LINGA LINGA LINGA—and then let loose, and he'd catch it in his mouth. He was a good recycler.

—Fernando, Mexico, b. 1958

At our Catholic school, it was an ongoing challenge to see how clever we could be in driving the nuns crazy. We learned early on to pick on their weaknesses. For example, there was an elderly nun who couldn't see very well. We discovered that we could aim our watches so that the glare would hit her right in the eyes. No matter where she was in the room, someone could get the angle just right. She'd be squinting and dodging, never realizing what was going on.

I played my all-time best grammar school prank on a nun who was particularly mean and nasty. She was a little bit nuts, so we decided to see if we could push her over the edge. I snuck out of class while her back was turned and ran downstairs smearing ketchup on my shirt. I ran outside and lay down on the grass under the classroom window. A classmate screamed, "Sister Loretta! Peter jumped out the window!" She looked down at me, shrieked, and made everyone leave the room. I changed into a fresh shirt I'd hidden, put my tie back on, and ran back upstairs. Meanwhile she went for the principal and a couple of other teachers, and when they didn't find me outside they ran back to the classroom, where we were all sitting at our desks as if nothing had happened. She practically fainted when she saw me sitting there. I got marched over to see the monsignor and ended up having to spend two weeks after school painting the convent basement. But it was worth it. It was more than worth it, because after that Sister Loretta eased up on us.

—Peter, New York, b. 1964

We had an orange tree in the yard and a dog named Hannibal who liked to chew the oranges until they were soggy. My friend Eric and I were bored and began lobbing mushy oranges over the high fence that separated our yard from our neighbor's. Soon there was a call from the neighbor who was screaming mad. They were having an engagement party out back and one of the oranges had knocked the hat off the 80-year-old maiden aunt. It turned out she was bald underneath, and no one had known until now. My mother made me go next door to apologize. Hannibal followed me over and when the neighbor answered the door and I was making my apology, Hannibal pushed past, sniffed the tea cart, raised his leg, and took a piss. To this day, Eric and I argue over who had the winning toss.

—Bob, California, b. 1957

78

When I was about thirteen I skipped a lot of school and found a use for my new low voice. I used to call my friends' parents and pretend I was a radio announcer calling from the local station. I'd offer lots of fabulous prizes if they could correctly answer the following questions— really juvenile stuff like, "How much time does the average adult spend on the toilet in a lifetime?" And they would think hard about it; you could almost hear how hard they were thinking, and I'd just be doing my best not to bust my gut laughing. Just in case you want to know, the prizes I offered were always very nice, like color TVs and trips. What can I say, I was evil.

—Allan, Ontario, b. 1947

I went to a Catholic grammar school in Brooklyn. In sixth grade, a future engineer in our class designed the ultimate device for duplicating the beautiful (to an eleven-year-old, at least) sound of human flatulence. This fart machine consisted of a short length of wire hanger with a rubber band attached at each end. You twisted the rubber band over and over and placed it in an envelope, and then sat on it, so that all you had to do was lift a cheek to produce the desired, highly realistic, audio effect. About a dozen of us began manufacturing these devices at a furious pace. In the classroom, someone would detonate one while the teacher was writing on the black-board. She would head back to find out who had done it, and someone else would let his go. Our teacher was a young nun who obviously was not cut out for teaching this age group, and she may have left teaching anyway, but I truly believe that the fart machines drove her to it. One day she just wasn't there anymore. I felt sad for her at the time, because she seemed so emotionally spent, but what can you do? Those fart machines were great!

—Steve, Brooklyn, b. 1958

My son insisted on getting some expensive athletic pants; he had to have them and so I relented and got them for him. They were made by Adidas or Nike in some shiny synthetic material. When they were brand new, he and his friends decided to amuse themselves by lighting their farts, and he caught his pants on fire. I couldn't believe it. He even got burns where the material melted onto his skin. From now on he can buy his own fancy pants.

—Wendy, about her son Aaron, Oregon, b. 1986

When I was eleven I used to take the train by myself from New York to Pennsylvania, to visit my grandmother on the weekends. Grandmother never drove, but she had a Model T for the handyman. I used it to drive my friends to the movies in the next town over. I would put on a grown man's hat, sit on some pillows, and drive the back roads to the movie house. I got arrested three times. Every time, Grandmother was the one who had to go to court, since I was there on the weekends only. By the third time, the judge had gotten to know her pretty well. He said to her, "Mrs. Browning, can't you just stop that boy from driving the car?" And she said, "Judge, even if he were your grand-son, he would still be driving." He said, "Fifty dollars," she paid it, and that was it. The cops ignored me after that.

—Pie, New York, b. 1909

A friend and I found a coffee can of gasoline in the garage and decided to pour some down a manhole, light it, and see what would happen. We popped the manhole open, poured some gas in, and replaced the cover so that it was ajar. We kept throwing matches down but nothing happened, so we poured all the gas in. Finally there was a noise like a jet engine starting up, and then a big boom! The manhole cover flew up and a flame shot up about fifteen feet in the air. The ground was rumbling like an earthquake, and the manhole cover crashed about twelve feet away in the neighbor's driveway. What happened was the gas ran down the sewer lines for a block or so and vaporized with all the methane in there, and blew up all our neighbors' toilets. I'm a plumber now; that's how I know exactly what happened.

—Dave, Washington, b. 1952

I spent hours poking at ant nests. I loved to watch them panic and start moving their eggs. One day it hit me that these eggs looked just like Rice Krispies, and I wondered what they would taste like. But I didn't want to taste one. So I collected a bunch of the eggs and put them in my big sister's bowl of Rice Krispies. She ate the whole bowl without ever noticing a thing. I decided that ants' eggs not only look like Rice Krispies, but taste like them, too. And the thing is, I liked my sister.

—Rick, North Carolina, b. 1955

As a young boy I loved sweets, including fruit—especially the guavas on our neighbor's tree. But the lady who lived there didn't want us kids eating all her guavas, so when they became ripe she was like a hawk, watching out her back window. All we could do was think about those ripening guavas. We invented a special tool, using a long forked stick with a rice bag hanging at the end, and a piece of bamboo across the opening that would pull the fruit off the branch and drop it into the bag. We camouflaged it with leaves and then snuck out when we were supposed to be napping during the heat of the day. In a few days, the tree was stripped. We were nearly sick, we were so full of guavas. We had to eat all of the evidence.

—Wasif, India, b. 1972

A friend of mine and I used to hang out at a construction site where they were building a big hotel. One day, when they had it all framed in and had installed the windows—hundreds of windows—we were watching a carpenter work and by mistake he broke a window. He acted like it was no big deal, they'd just replace it. The next day was Saturday, and I went back there with a little idea in my head. I threw a stone through a window and when I heard that tinkling sound, there was no going back. I popped another one. It sounded soooooo good. By the fourth or fifth one I realized that they'd never think the carpenter had broken all these windows, but I figured they'd blame it on some other boys, the bad boys. Well, sure enough, by the end of the weekend ten or fifteen boys had been through there, and there wasn't a single window left intact. At one point I realized that it was really getting out of hand, but I couldn't stop it. And I had started it all. I figured that when they found out, I'd go to jail for life. I stopped eating, I couldn't sleep, I was so worried. I made a deal with myself: If I can get out of this somehow, I'll never get into trouble again. And I didn't. Well, mostly.

—Ron, Oregon, b. 1937

When we were young we looked up to the teenage boys who hung around the monument in the square at the center of town. We'd do anything for them—deliver messages, get cigarettes—so they wouldn't make us get lost. They would tell us, "Go find out what color underwear such-and-such a girl wears." So a couple of us would roll around on the ground wrestling until we got directly in the path of the girl, right underneath her skirt. If the girl knew our mothers, she'd tell, and we'd be crucified. The underpants were always white, but we made up colors to make a bigger impression.

—Ciro, Italy, b. 1956

When I was in junior high we took some tennis balls, soaked them in gasoline, and then lit them on fire and played night soccer in our driveway. My parents were out somewhere. The next morning they pulled me out of bed to come explain what had happened. There were scorch marks all over the garage door and melted globs of tennis ball in the driveway. I said, "Gee, I don't know, but I did hear some noises while I was sleeping." They didn't buy it; I was grounded for the next six weekends.

—Bruce, New Jersey, b. 1959

At school—in class or in the library—we used to catch flies for pets. We'd cup our hands and clap them over the fly so that it was stunned but not dead. We would take a long hair from a girl in class and tie it around the fly's leg very carefully. (Don't ask me how we did this; I think we must have severed a lot of legs.) Then we'd wait till the fly came to its senses and took off, while we were holding the hair. It would fly in circles, around and around, and kids would start to laugh and we'd get in trouble.

—John, Connecticut, b. 1959

There was a guy in the neighborhood who would catch bumblebees and put them in the freezer for a while until they went dormant. Then we'd tie thread around their middles. It was always a race to get this done before they thawed out. (Don't let anyone tell you that bumblebees don't sting.) We held the spool of thread and let them fly in circles, higher and higher, like a kite.

—Roger, Washington, b. 1950

We would collect cicadas in a jar and shake it up really hard. Then when we let them out they would fly like drunks.

—Gilberto, Brazil, b. 1944

We had a shower stall with a glass door, and one time I decided to see how much water it could hold. I stopped up the drain and turned on the water full blast and shut the door. Then I sat there and watched it fill up. When it was almost all the way to the top, the glass blew out of the door, in slow motion, like a special effect. I didn't get cut, but I got soaked.

—Casey, Utah, b. 1956

My cousins lived in our neighborhood. They were
my best friends and we played together every day.
The only problem was that whenever I went over
there, we always had to do some chore before we
were allowed to run off. So one day I went over
to play football, but we had to clean up all
these leaves and newspapers in the yard beside the
house before we could play. I had the brainstorm
of lighting it on fire. That way, we
could go off and play and the job would get done
by itself. So we lit it and took off, and the house
caught on fire. It's really terrible when you do
that to your own relatives. You have to face them
at every family gathering for the rest of your life.

—Eddie, New Jersey, b. 1960

KEY TO OVERLEAF

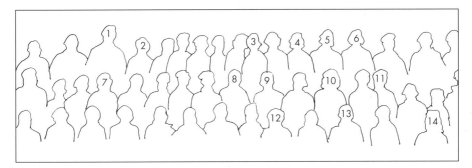

1. Put fish in water cooler
2. Threw Jell-O bombs at girls
3. Used peashooter at Memorial Day parade
4. Lit smoke bombs in school bathroom
5. Unscrewed neighbors' Christmas tree lights
6. Smeared butter on car door handles
7. Rang doorbells and ran
8. Ate worms
9. Put chalk in erasers
10. Made underarm fart noises
11. Tied little sister's shoelaces together
12. Put potato in car exhaust
13. Put cornflakes in grandmother's bed
14. Champion spitter